This book belongs to:

_____

Match the Carnivore to it's shadow

Red Fox

Grizzly Bear

Gray Wolf

Canada Lynx

Over a dozen different types of carnivores live within Yellowstone.

Match the Rodent to it's shadow

Red Squirel

Beaver

Yellow-Bellied
Marmot

Chipmunk

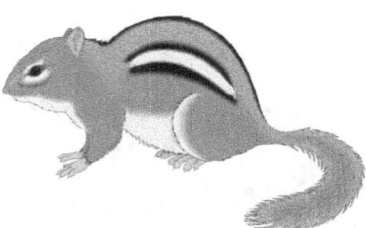

All rodents have a pair of incisors (teeth) that continue to grow throughout their lives, which they wear down through chewing.

Match the Carnivore to it's shadow

Badger

Black Bear

Bobcat

Coyote

Carnivores eat primarily meat.

Match the Ungulate to it's shadow

Bison

Bighorn Sheep

Elk

Moose

Ungulates are hooved herbivores (plant-eaters).

Match the Bird to it's shadow

Bald Eagle

Osprey

Great Horned Owl

Raven

Records of bird sightings have been kept in Yellowstone since its establishment in 1872.

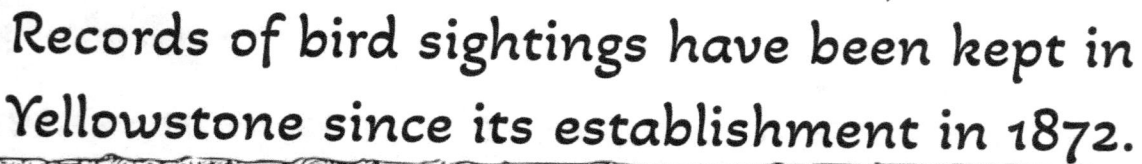

Match the Carnivore to it's shadow

Cougar

Long Tailed
Weasel

Marten

River Otter

Carnivores play an important role in the
greater Yellowstone Ecosystem.

WHAT'S MISSING?

CAMPING SHADOW MATCHING

PUZZLE TIME

WHAT DO THEY NEED?

CAMPING SHADOW MATCHING

HAIRY WOODPECKER

Woodpecker's bills help distribute shock throughout the thick skull when pecking.

THE GROTTO GEYSER

This geyser may have gotten it's unique shape from a trees stump that is covered with mineral deposits.

YELLOWSTONE
NATIONAL PARK
— WYOMING —

YELLOWSTONE SULFER BUCKWHEAT

This flower only grows in slightly geothermal areas within the park and nowhere else in the world.

YELLOWSTONE
NATIONAL PARK
—— WYOMING ——

Help the river otter get back to his family.

Help the chipmunk get to the top of the tree.

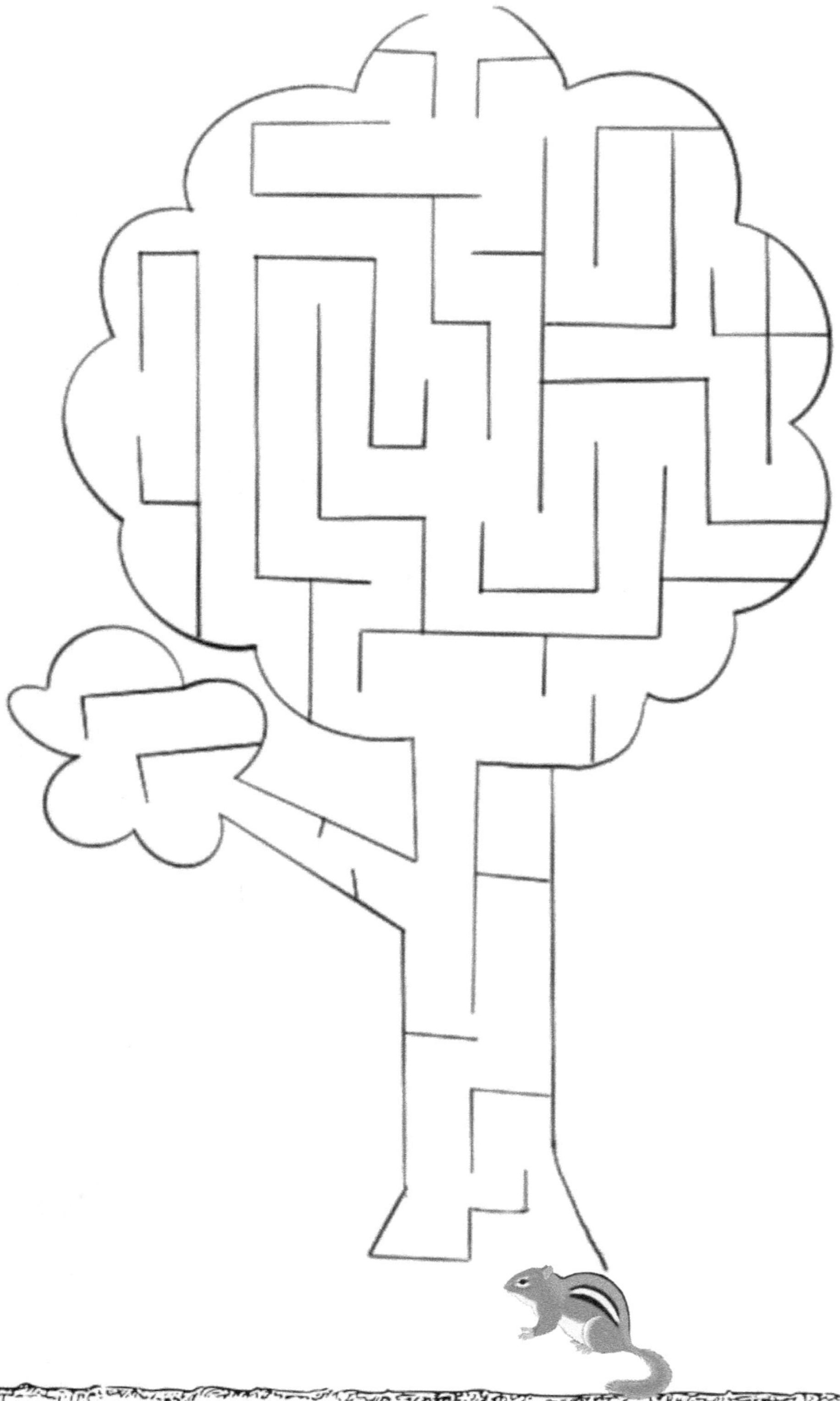

Help the bison get to Hayden Valley.

Help the lynx get back to her den.

Help the moose get to the mountains.

Help the
hiker get
back to her
cabin.

Help the butterfly get through the flower.

Camping

WHERE ARE THEY GOING?

PUZZLE TIME

HELP THE ANIMALS CHOOSE THE RIGHT WAY TO GET TO THE LAKE

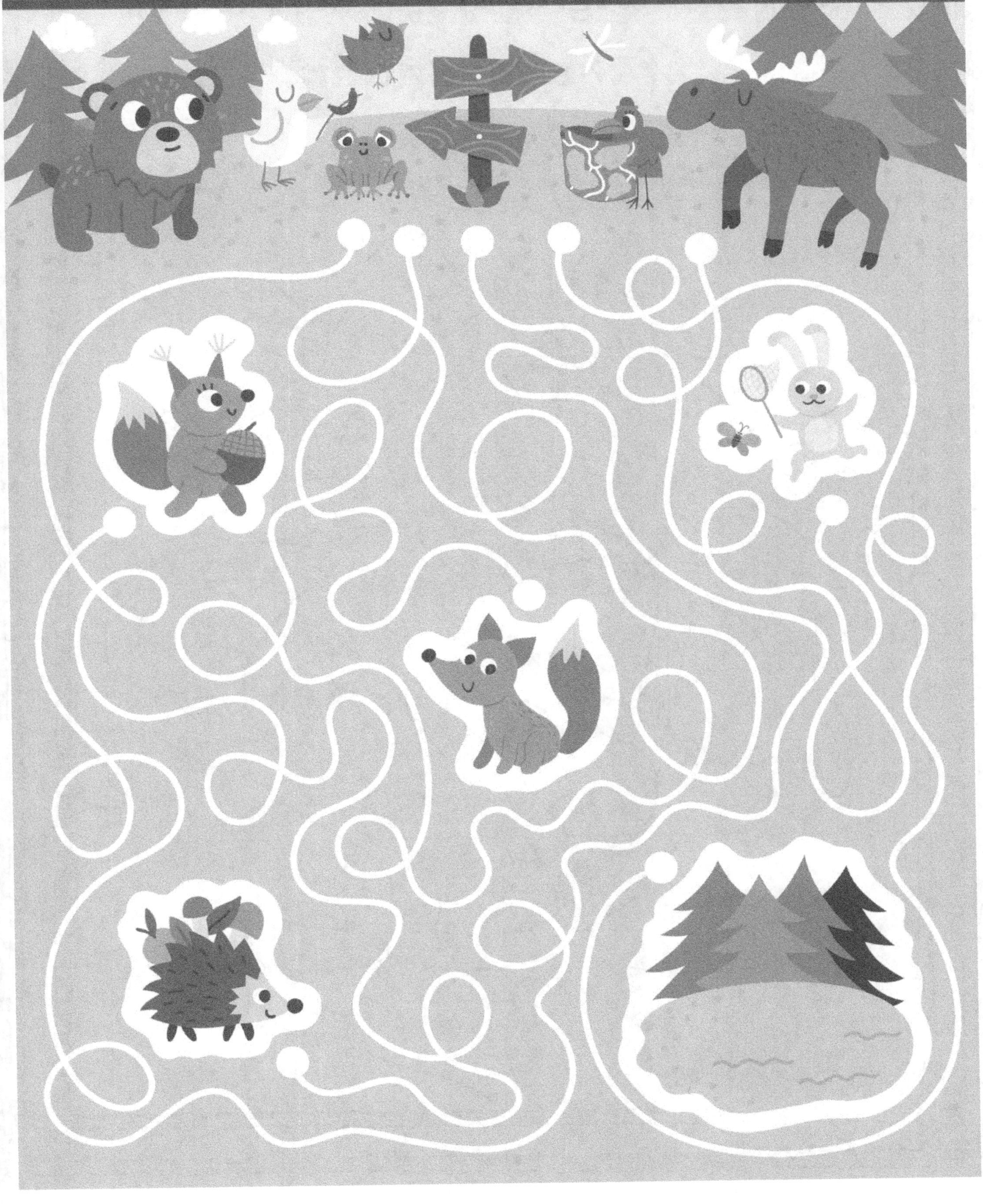

Help the bighorn get to the top of the mountain.

Boardwalks are for vistors safety and to preserve the park's natural features. It's important to stay on them at all times.

RIVER OTTER

Otters are excellent swimmers
and live primarily near rivers.

Maps are excellent ways of navigating through natural areas.

OLD FAITHFUL

Old Faithful was the first named geyser in the park.

HELP THE BUS GET TO THE CAMP

HELP THE ANIMALS CHOOSE
THE RIGHT WAY TO GET TO THE LAKE

HELP THE GIRL GET TO THE FIRE

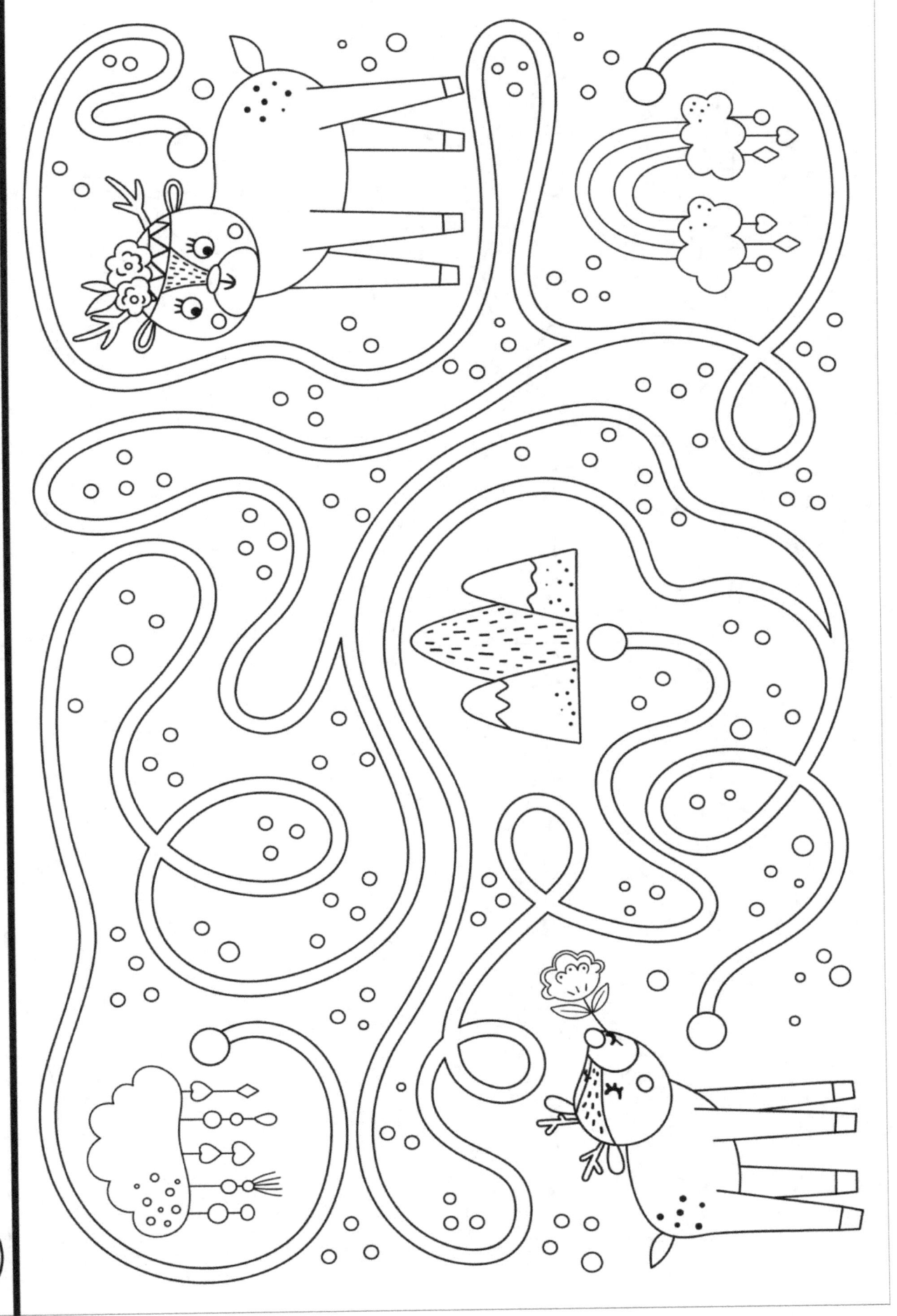

HELP BABY FOX FIND HIS MOM

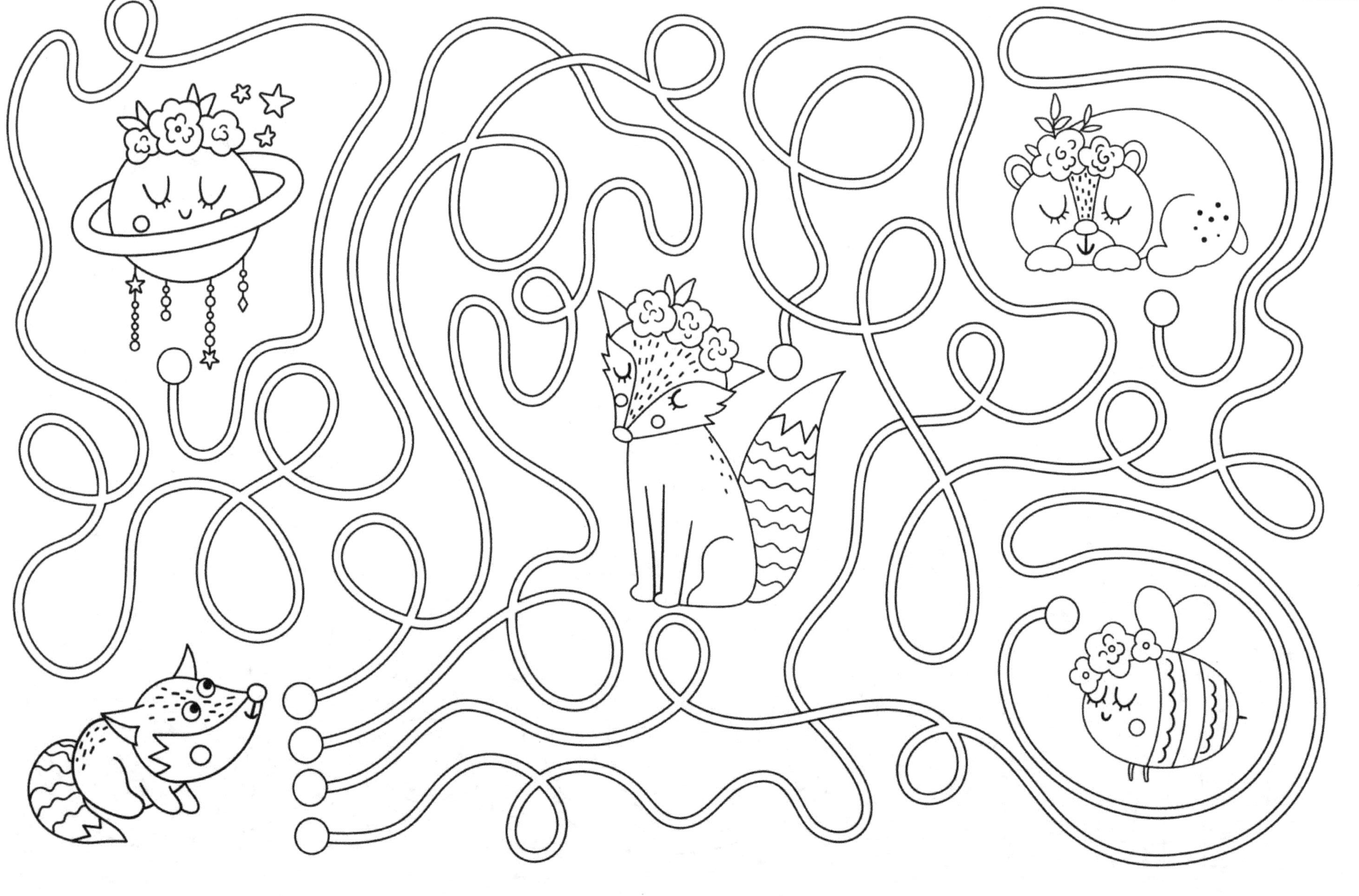

WHERE ARE THEY GOING?

Camping

WHO GOT THE FISH?

Create your own National Park Badge

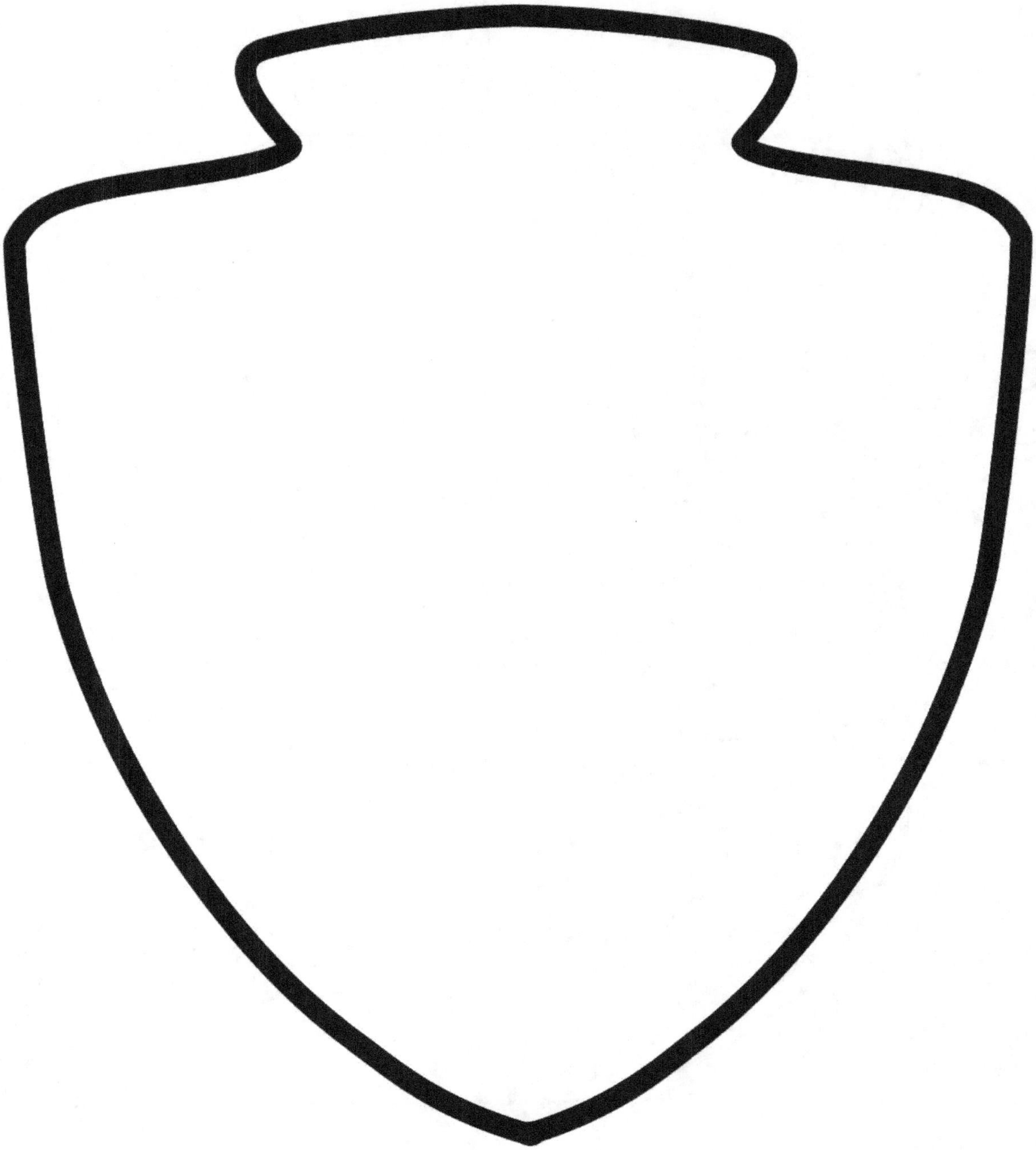

RED FOX

Red Foxes tails make up over half their total body length.

MOOSE

Bull moose usually shed their antlers in the beginning of winter to help conserve energy and survive the winter.

WOLVERINE

Wolverines have a keen sense of smell that can detect a dead animal 20 feet under the snow.

Find 7 differences between the pictures.

Find 5 differences between the pictures.

Find 5 differences between the pictures.

Spot 10 differences

PUZZLE TIME

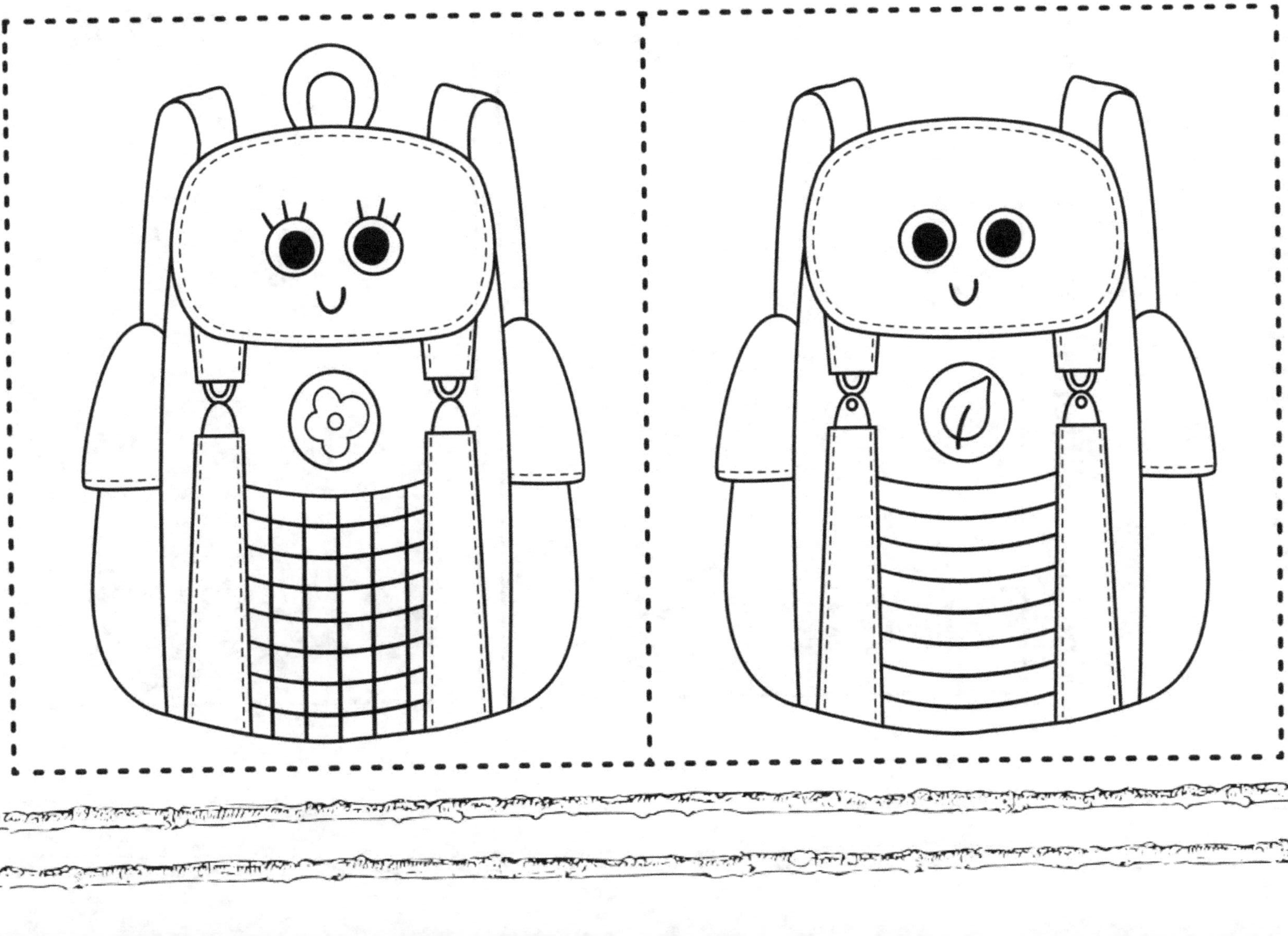

Find the difference

Hiking is a great way to get exercise and to see nature up close.

Find the 7 differences in the pictures below

Find the difference

Baby deer are called fawns and are born with white spots on their fur.

Find the 7 differences in the pictures below

Find the difference

Dragonflies spend most of their lives living as naiads under the water.

Find the 7 differences in the pictures below

It can get windy around the boardwalks. Make sure to hold onto your hats while visiting. Over 400 hats are lost a year in the park.

PRESIDENT ROOSEVELT

President Roosevelt did not establish Yellowstone as a National Park, but his name is tied to the park due to his long journey here and commitment to setting aside lands for public use.

Nearly 300 species of birds call Yellowstone home.

134 butterfly varieties exist
within Yellowstone.

Pattern Completion
Circle or Draw the object that comes next

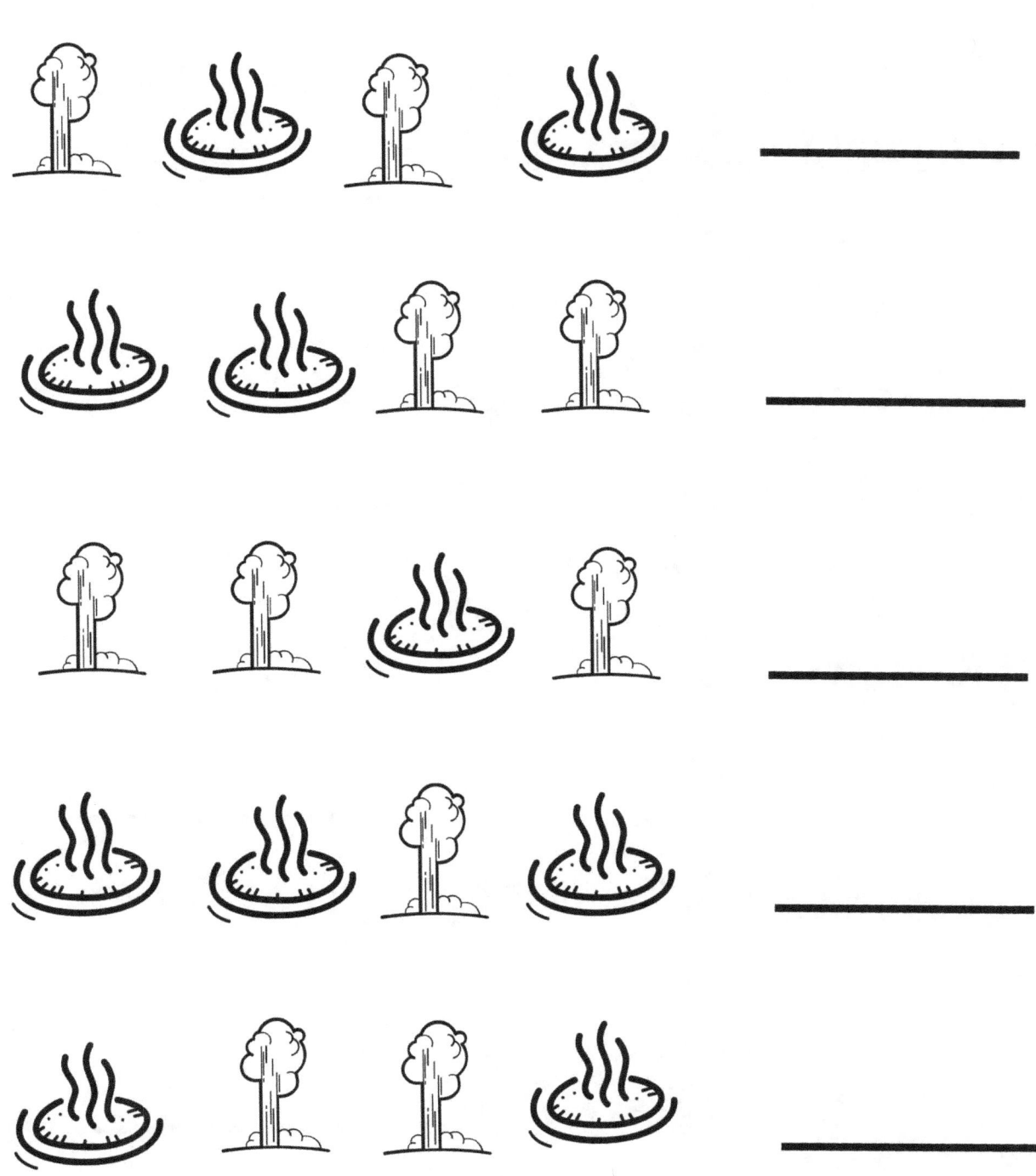

Pattern Completion
Circle or Draw the object that comes next

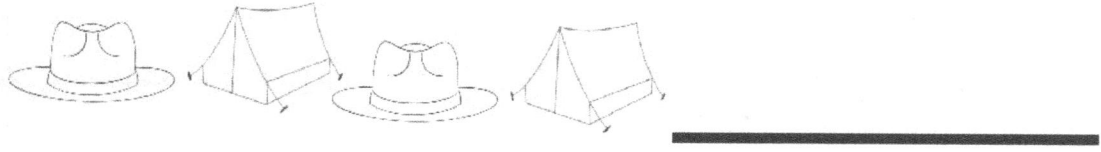

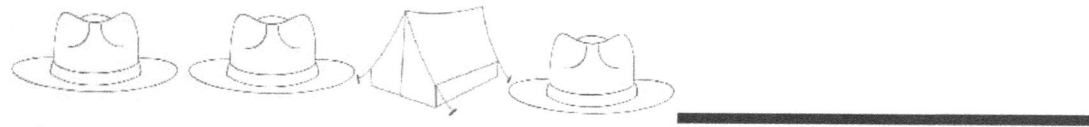

Pattern Completion
Circle or Draw the object that comes next

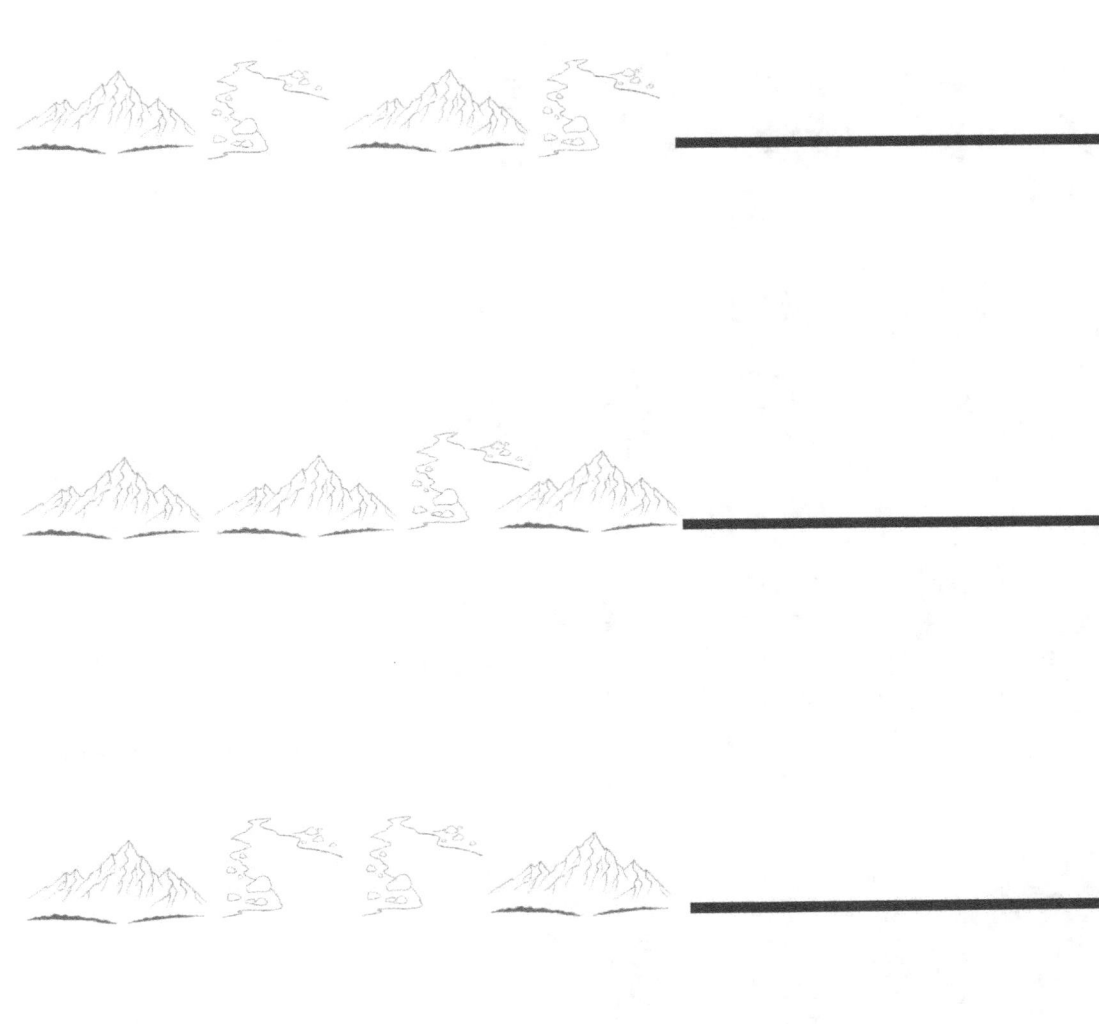

Pattern Completion
Circle or Draw the object that comes next

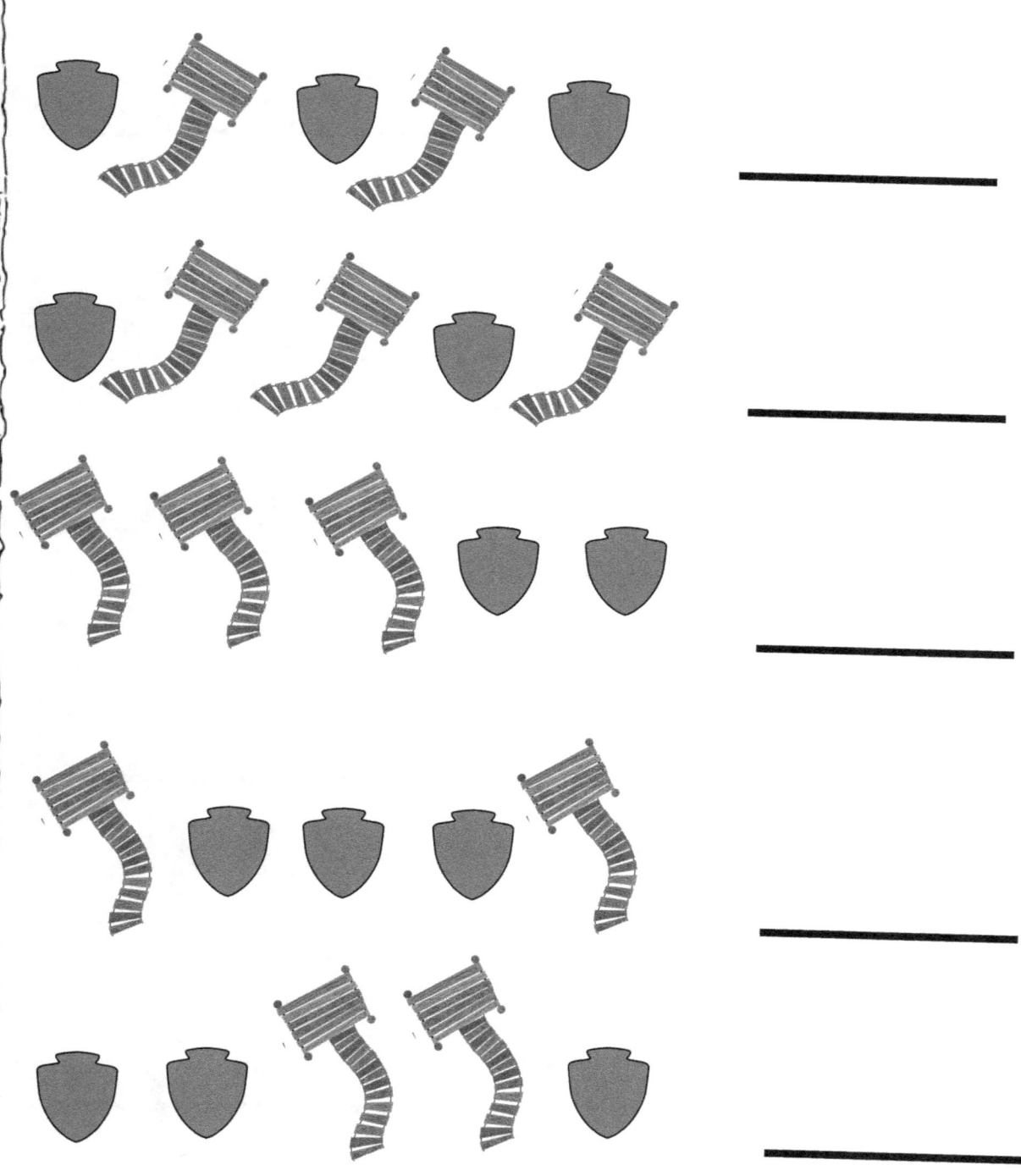

_____

_____

_____

_____

_____

Pattern Completion
Circle or Draw the object that comes next

Pattern Completion
Circle or Draw the object that comes next

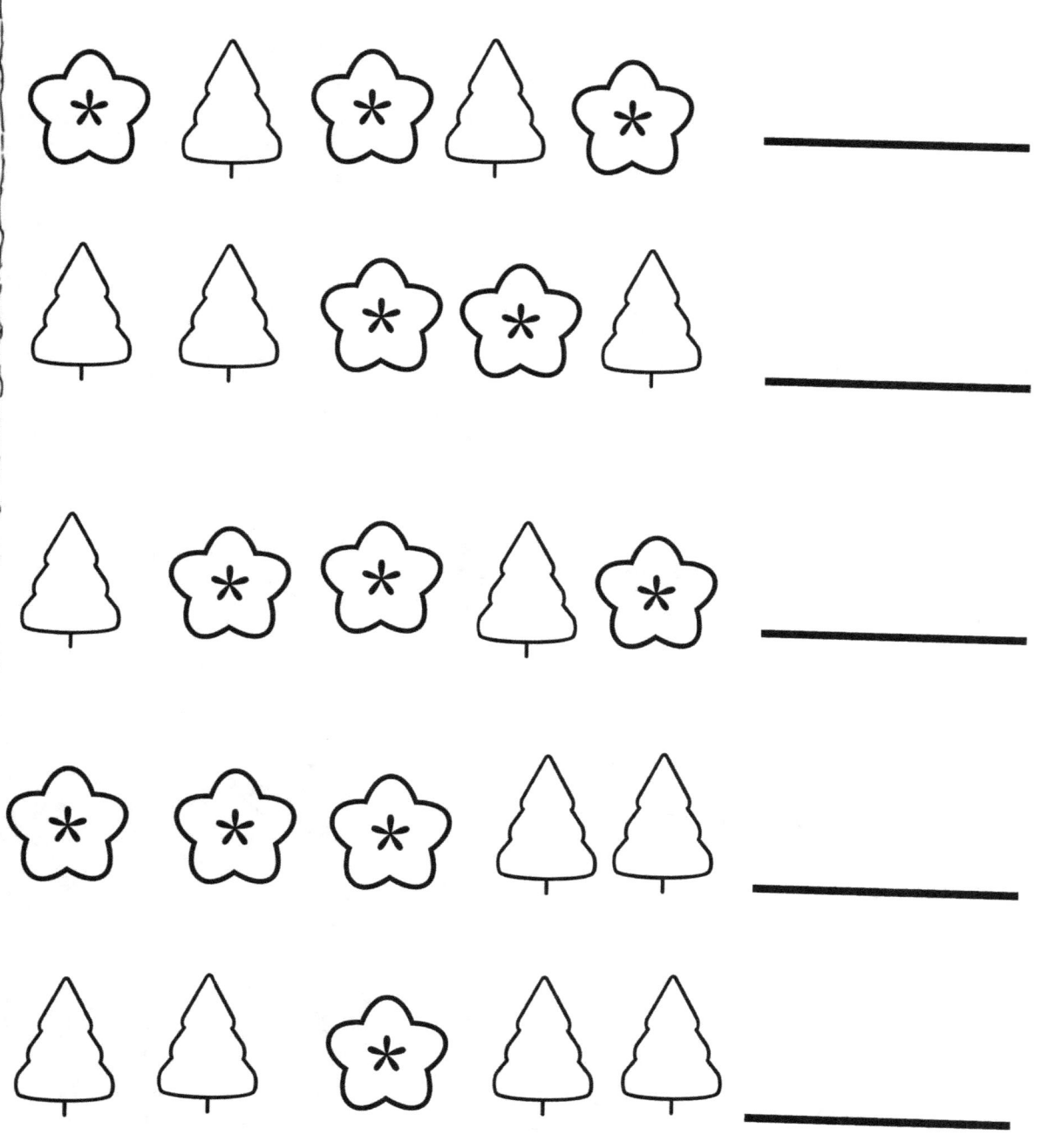

SHOOTING STAR FLOWER

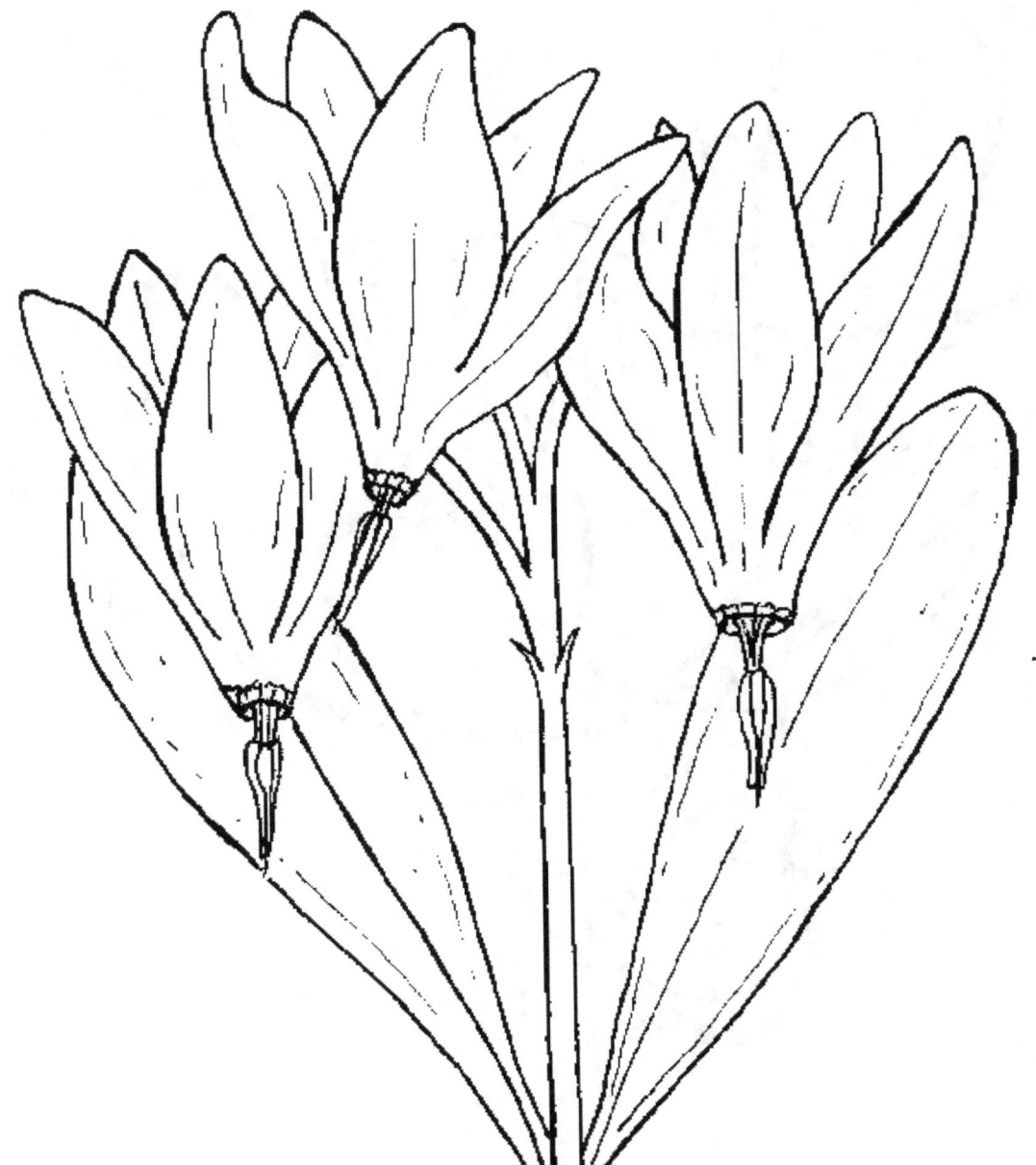

These vibrant purple flowers can be found in meadow areas of the park.

Did you know there are cactus in Yellowstone? Look for these bright yellow flowers on Plains Pricklypear Cactus near Mammoth and Snake River.

Cougar

Cougars have many names including, mountain lion, puma, panther, or catamount.

HIKING

Be sure to be "Bear Aware" when hiking in the park. Always travel in at least groups of three and make lots of noise while hiking.

How many Grizzly Bears can you find?

A surprising food source for grizzly's is moths.
They can eat up to 40,000 moths a day!

CAMPING SEEK AND FIND

find the objects in the picture

How many bison can you find?

Bison cause traffic jams regularly at the park.

How many Moose can you find?

Moose are pretty fast swimmers. They have been observed swimming long distances – over ten miles – in search of food and good habitat.

How many River Otters can you find?

Otters have a great way to get around. Sliding! They drop on their belly and slide in the snow and ice.

How many Mule Deer can you find?

Mule deer get their name from their big, mule-like ears.

How many owls can you find?
The fir and spruce forests of the park make an ideal habitat for owls.

Fly fishing for trout is an very popular activity
in Yellowstone's Rivers.

MORNING GLORY

Morning glory used to be entirely blue, but because of changing water tempature, it is now green, yellow and orange.

Bison

Bison are the largest mammal in North America.

GRAND CANYON OF THE YELLOWSTONE

The park gets it's name from the yellow sandstones along the banks of the Yellowstone River.

I SPY

 — ❓    — ❓    — ❓

 — ❓    — ❓   — ❓

 — ❓    — ❓    — ❓

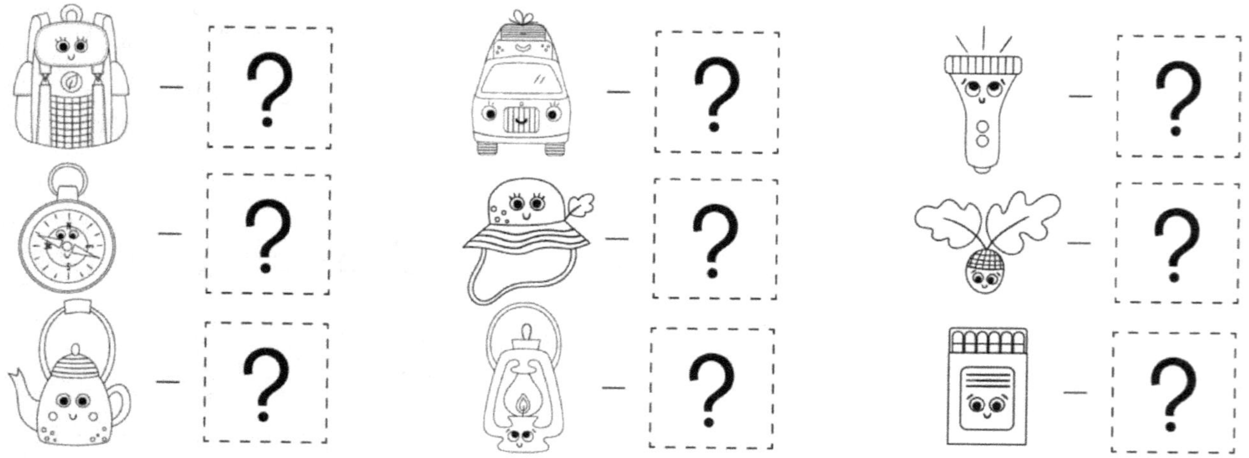

I SPY

 — **?**  — **?**  — **?**  — **?**

 — **?**  — **?**  — **?** 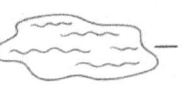 — **?**

 — **?**  — **?**  — **?** 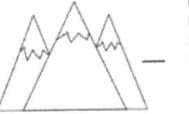 — **?**

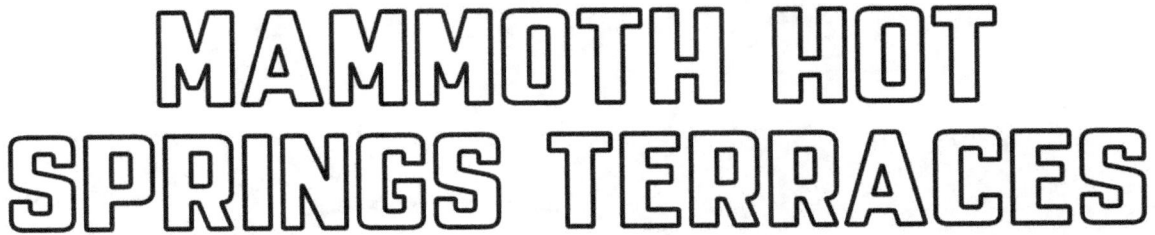

MAMMOTH HOT SPRINGS TERRACES

Mammoth Hot Springs has been described as looking like a cave turned inside out.

LOWER
YELLOWSTONE FALLS

Connect the Dots

BEAVER

A family of beavers is called a Colony. There are over 100 colonies of beavers in Yellowstone.

RIVER OTTER

A group of otters can be called a family, romp or raft. Which do you like best?

Connect the Dots

11

10

8

13

12

6

9

7

15

5

14

17

4

16

3

18

2

19

20

1

Connect the Dots

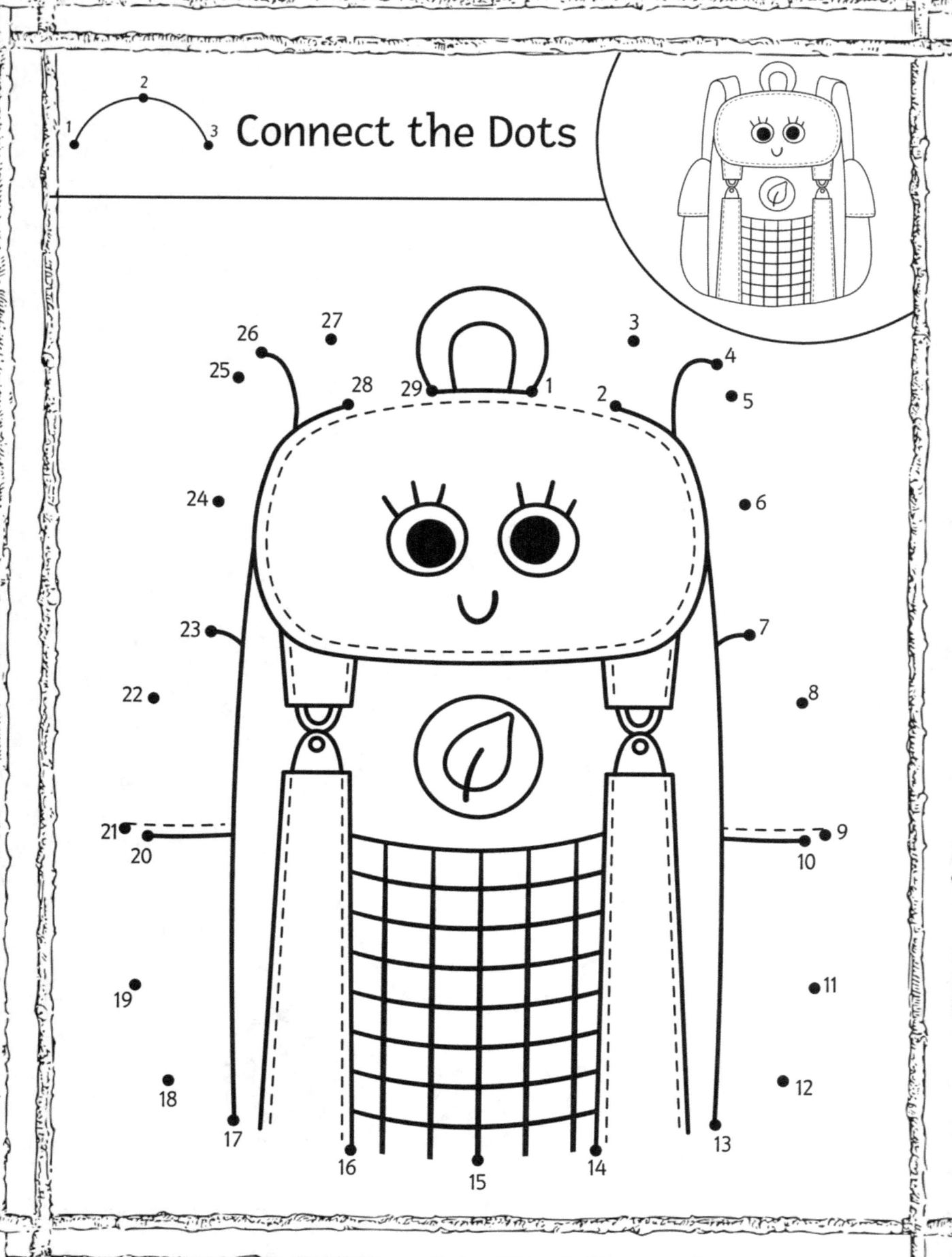

GRAY WOLF

A group of wolves is called a pack. There are estimated to be 8 packs of wolves living in Yellowstone.

LONG TAILED WEASEL

A group of weasels can be called a colony, gang or pack.

BOBCAT

A group of bobcats is called a clowder, clutter or pounce.

Ranger Hat

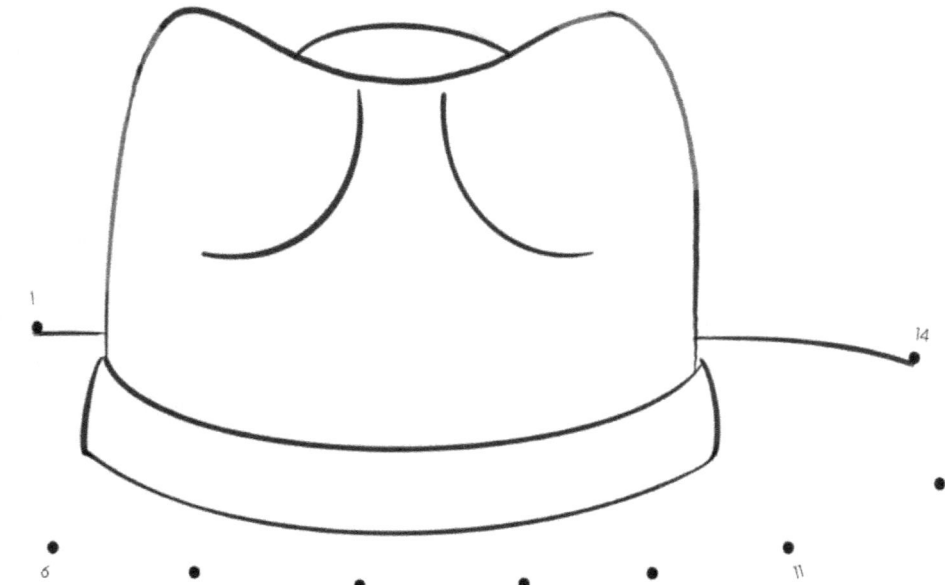

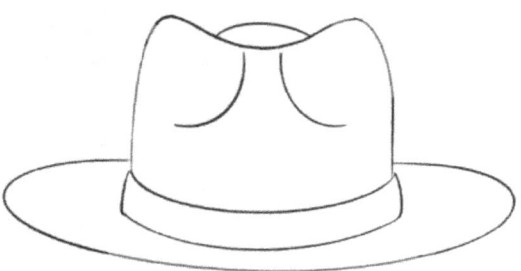

What would you call a group of Park Rangers?

Red Fox

A group of foxes is called a skulk or a leash.

Mule Deer

A group of mule deer is called a herd.

BIGHORN SHEEP

A group of bighorn sheep is called a herd.

GRAY WOLF

The coat color of wolves in
Yellowstone can be black or gray.

Tic Tac Toe

Challenge your friends and family!

Example:

Tic Tac Toe

Challenge your friends and family!

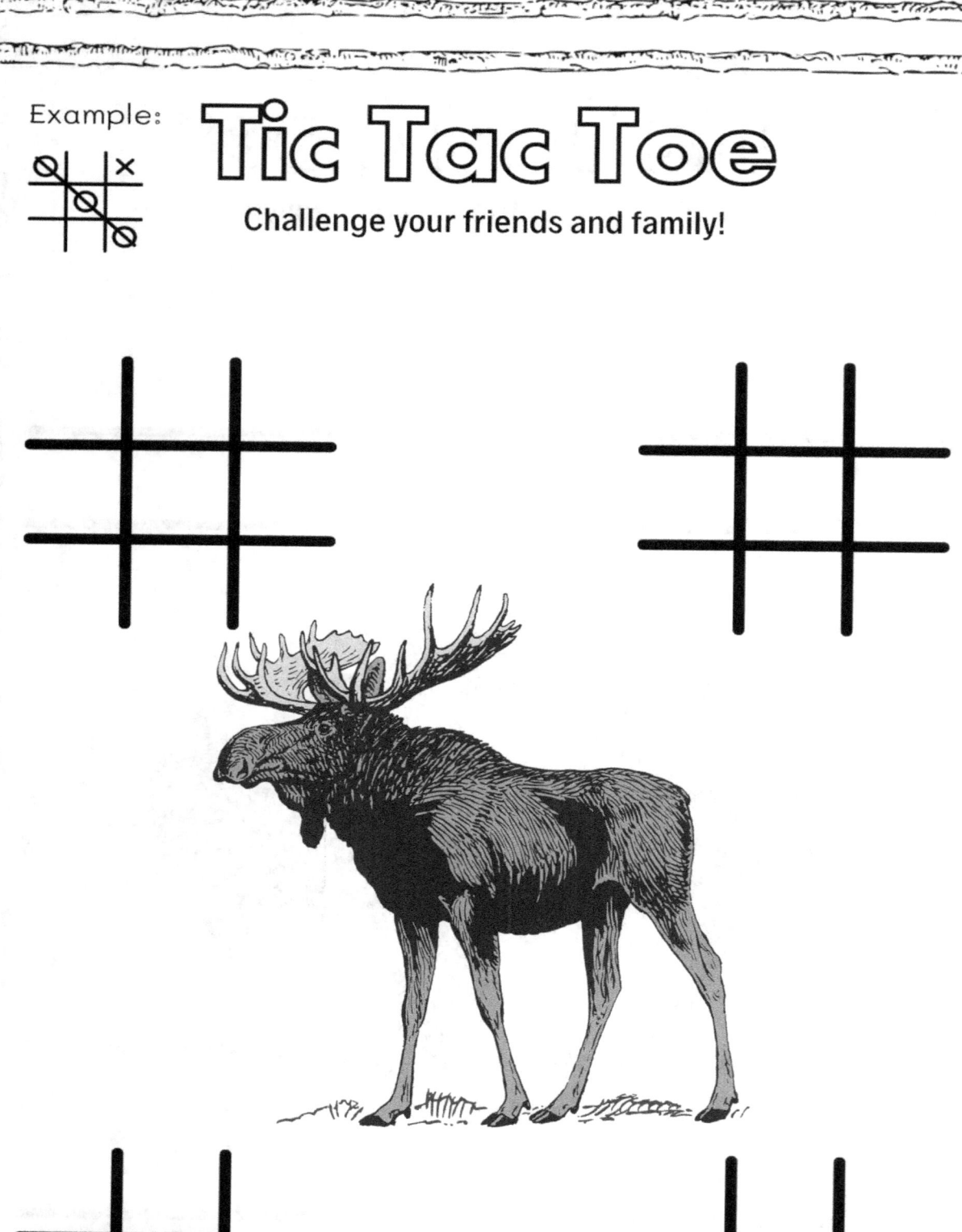

Example:

Tic Tac Toe

Challenge your friends and family!

Example: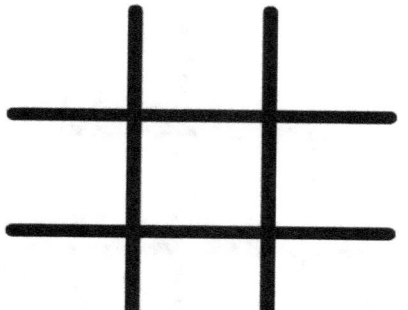

Tic Tac Toe

Challenge your friends and family!

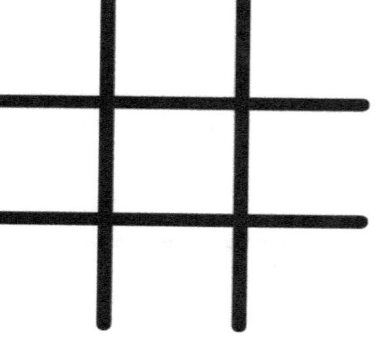

Tic Tac Toe

Challenge your friends and family!

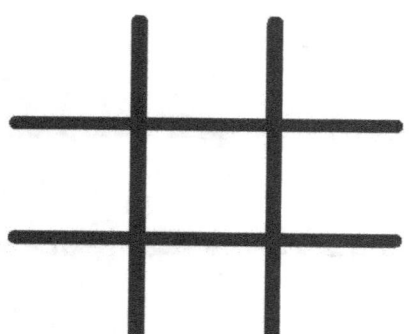

Tic Tac Toe
Challenge your friends and family!

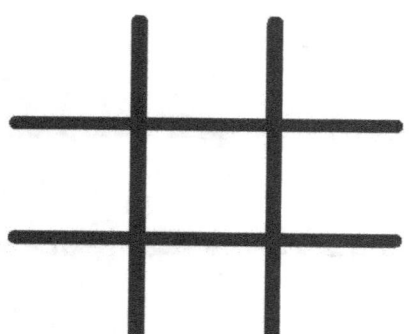

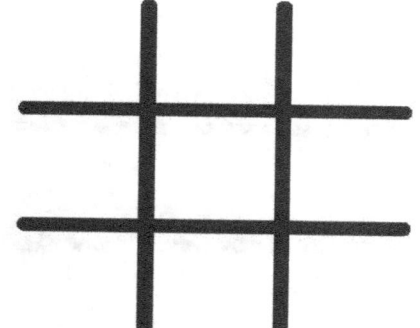

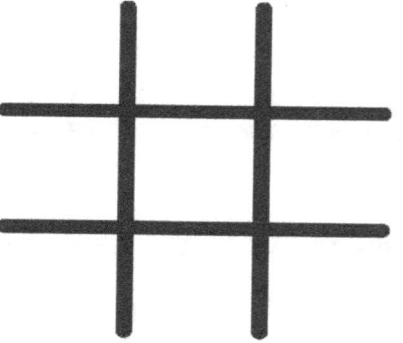

Drawing Practice
Draw Eyes on the Owl

Owls are nocturnal, which means they sleep during the day and are active at night.

Drawing Practice

Draw antlers on the Mule Deer

Example

Deer have antlers, which is a bone connected to their skull bone and are shed each year and regrown.

Drawing Practice

Draw Horns in the BigHorn Sheep

Example

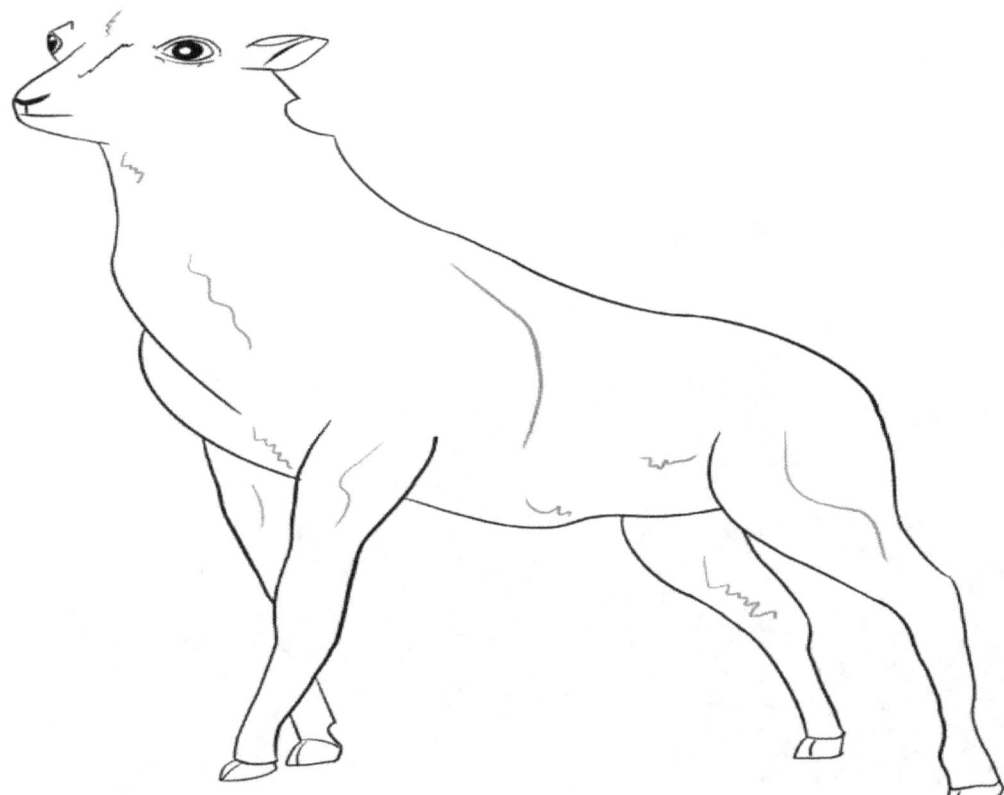

Horns are part bone and specialized hair follicles (similar to human fingernails), and are not shed like antlers.

Drawing Practice
Draw a Geyser Erupting

Not all geysers are predictable, some erupt frequently (every 90 minutes) and some only every few years.

Drawing Practice
Draw hikers on the hill

Make sure to be prepared for hiking: Good shoes, plenty of water and a map.

Drawing Practice
Draw a hat on the ranger

Rangers have two main responsibilities:
Protect the park and visitors to the park.

GRAND PRISMATIC SPRING

This spring is so large, it's best to hike up to the platform to see it from above.

BOREAL CHORUS FROG

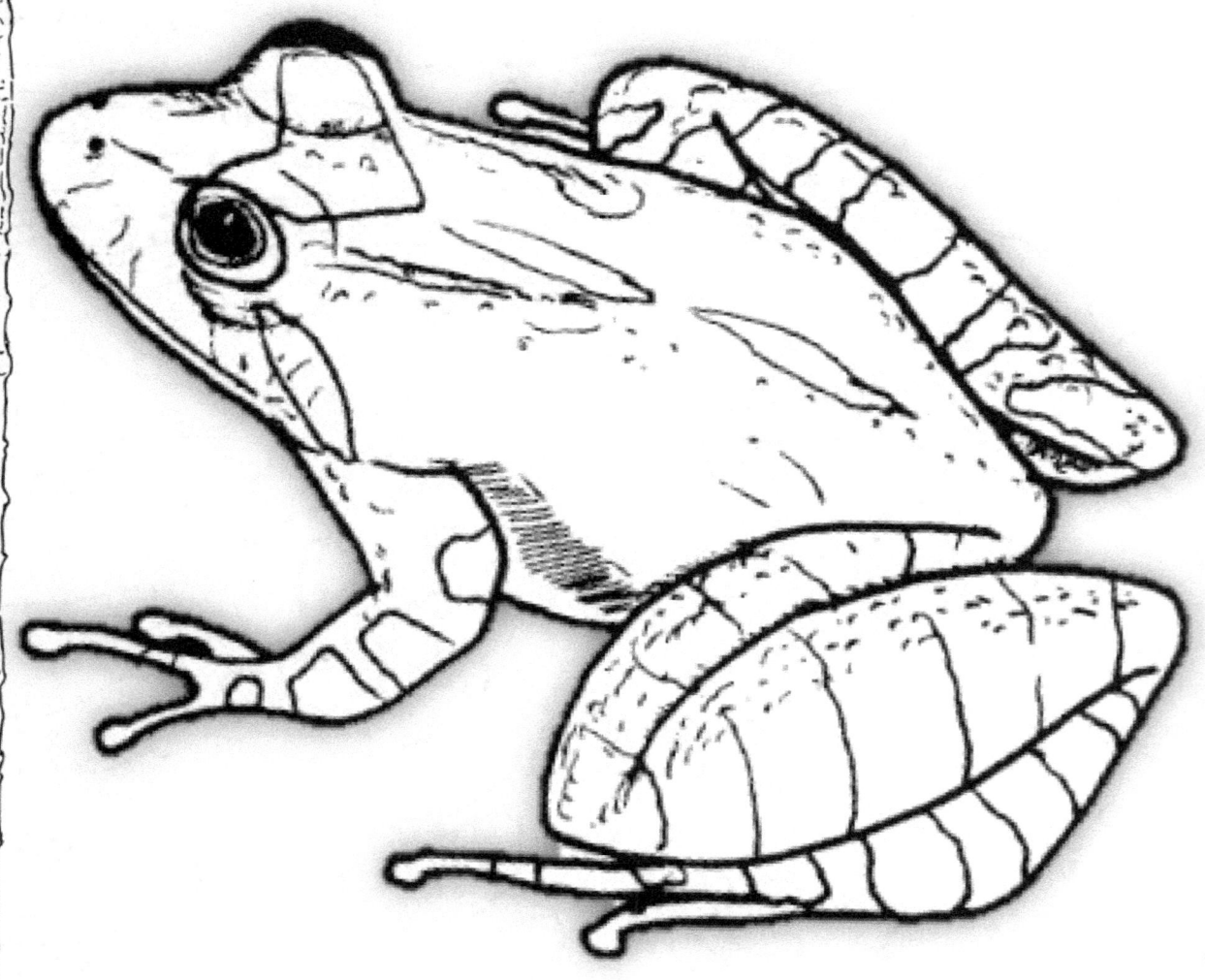

These frogs are often heard, but rarely seen.
Adults usually don't get longer than 1.5 inches.

Bald Eagle

Bald eagles are usually found near water where they feed on fish and waterfowl. They also generally nest in large trees close to water.